The Corporate Mentor's Toolkit: Transforming Teams and Organizations

Kostiantyn Koptelov

The Corporate Mentor's Toolkit: Transforming Teams and Organizations by Kostiantyn Koptelov

Contents

About the book, what is mentoring, and why is it needed .. 7

Mentoring as a tool for development 10

    Key principles of mentoring 11

    Objectives of the Mentoring Program 12

    What is the difference between Mentoring and Coaching and Tutoring 14

    Roles in the Mentoring Program 16

        Mentor. 16

        Human Resources. 17

    FAQ for mentor... 19

        What does a mentor get out of working with a mentee?... 19

        What effect does a mentor have? 19

        Where can a mentor get helpful information?........... 19

        Is it possible for a mentor to have their mentor?....... 20

        How many mentees can one mentor have? 20

        How does a mentor report on work completed? 20

        Is it necessary to follow the algorithms and forms in this book? 20

Requests for mentorship and what to do 22

Criteria for the formation of pairs of mentor-mentee..... 26

Key stages of the program... 28

    Key stages of the mentoring program: 28

    The frequency of the interaction................................ 28

    Interaction formats 29

The Corporate Mentor's Toolkit: Transforming Teams and Organizations by Kostiantyn Koptelov

- Reverse mentoring 30
- Mentor-mentee interaction 32
  - The scenario of getting acquainted 33
  - The scenario of a regular meeting with a mentee 36
  - Scenarios of the final meeting to summarize the results of the program 40
  - Important forms 43
- Examples of homework for mentee's soft skills development 49
  - Effective communication 50
    - Option 1. Let's start the dialogue with the proper preparation 50
    - Option 2. Reading list 51
  - Strategic mindset 53
    - Option 1. Scenario planning 53
    - Option 2. Play games 53
    - Option 3. Highlight possible risks 54
    - Option 4. Zoom in 54
    - Option 5. Reading list 55
  - Decision making 56
    - Option 1. Descartes Square 56
    - Option 2. Method of pairwise comparison of solutions 57
    - Option 3. Method of comparing decisions by criteria 58
    - Option 4. SWOT Analysis 59
    - Option 5. Reading list 60
  - Public speaking 61

The Corporate Mentor's Toolkit: Transforming Teams and Organizations by Kostiantyn Koptelov

- Option 1. Elevator pitch 61
- Option 2. Learn to answer questions using the principle of "thesis, argument, proof." 62
- Option 3. Analysis of public speaking 63
- Option 4. Speak 63
- Option 5. Use Simon Sinek's method 64

Time management 65
- Option 1. Prioritization by importance and urgency .. 65
- Option 2. Kanban Task Management Board 66
- Option 3. Retrospective 69
- Option 4. Reading list 70

Influence 71
- Option 1. Analyze the successful experience of your colleagues 71
- Option 2. Improve your emotional intelligence 72
- Option 3. Boost your self-confidence 72
- Option 4. Reading list 73

Stress management 74
- Option 1. Start by planning for rest and recovery 74
- Option 2. Analyze stressors and emotional swings .. 75
- Option 3. Clarification of meaning 76
- Option 4. Prepare for stress 76
- Option 5. Finding your way to work with stress 77

Key mentoring skills 78
- Making contact 79
- Active listening 81

The Corporate Mentor's Toolkit: Transforming Teams and Organizations by Kostiantyn Koptelov

- Active Listening Techniques 81
- Developmental feedback 84
  - Principles of developmental feedback: 84
  - Feedback schemes 85
- Reframing 87
  - Context reframing 88
  - Showing the other side 88
  - Reframing with "But" 89
  - Reframing with connotations 89
  - Use of an alternative question 89
- Asking developmental questions 91
  - Examples of questions 92
- Ability to explain and instruct clearly 94
  - The principle of hierarchy (the pyramid) 94
  - The principle of "starting from the needs of the mentee" 95
  - The principle of "from bump to bump" 95
  - The principle of "thesis - argument - proof" .. 96
- Setting developmental goals 97
  - SMART model 97
  - OKR Model 99
- Assistance in development planning 100
  - Stage GOAL 100
  - Stage REALITY 101
  - Stage OPTIONS/OBSTACLES 102
  - Stage WAY FORWARD 103

Ability to inspire and challenge 105
  Tactic 1: Help the mentee feel the meaning of the work 105
  Tactic 2. Communicate 106
  Tactic 3. Maintain corporate culture and traditions . 106
  Tactic 4. Explain and, at the same time, give emotions 106
  Tactic 5. Use the SCARF pyramid 107
Final words 109

The Corporate Mentor's Toolkit: Transforming Teams and Organizations by Kostiantyn Koptelov

About the book, what is mentoring, and why is it needed

Hi!

My name is Konstantin Koptelov. And I invite you to figure out how to become a first-class corporate mentor within the company mentorship program. You can, of course, use the skills you learn outside of your company. Still, the book is written in a way that makes it as likely as possible that you will use the skills you learn to help your colleagues grow and develop.

We will deal with the following:

1. What is mentoring, and how does it differ from coaching and management?
2. Who is a mentor?
3. Why do they need to participate in the mentoring program?
4. What essential skills should they have?
5. How to develop them?
6. How to choose a mentee?
7. What can be the scenarios of the interaction between mentor and mentee?
8. What skills do your mentee develop, and how can you help them to do that?
9. What homework can you give to your mentee?
10. How do you get the most out of your mentoring program?

The Corporate Mentor's Toolkit: Transforming Teams and Organizations by Kostiantyn Koptelov

You will get a large set of tools, scenarios, tasks, and skills to be fully prepared to be a professional corporate mentor.

Participation in the program will allow you to develop yourself very strongly and enjoy the way you help another person become better.

Good luck on your way to becoming a professional mentor!

The Corporate Mentor's Toolkit: Transforming Teams and Organizations by Kostiantyn Koptelov

Disclaimer:

This book is meant to give you information, not legal advice, so don't take it that way. The information in this book comes from the author's research and personal experience. Still, it might not be complete or up-to-date. The use of brand names in this book is only to show examples. It does not mean that the author supports or is affiliated with the brand. The author and publisher make no promises or warranties, either express or implied, about the book or its information, products, services, or graphics being complete, accurate, reliable, suitable, or available for any purpose. Any reliance you place on such information is, therefore, strictly at your own risk. In no case will the author or publisher be responsible for any loss or damage, including, but not limited to, indirect or consequential loss or damage, or any loss or damage at all caused by the loss of data or profits resulting from or related to the use of this book. If a brand name or trademark is mentioned in this book, it is up to the reader to get permission to use it.

The Corporate Mentor's Toolkit: Transforming Teams and Organizations by Kostiantyn Koptelov

Mentoring as a tool for development

Mentoring is a type of informal coaching. Its goal is to give employees chances to improve themselves, their leadership skills, and their potential. It also makes it easier for a new worker to jump right into the work process and helps build a corporate culture. Mentoring is part of the training of the new generation of managers.

A mentor is usually an experienced employee who helps a mentee improve their skills and career by sharing their knowledge, skills, and time. They act as a "role model" for their mentee.

In this part, we will find out what the fundamental principles of mentoring are and try to answer the most common questions about the mentoring program.

Let's start!

Key principles of mentoring

Fundamental principles of mentoring:
1. Respect – participants of the program show tolerance for a point of view that differs from their own;
2. Purposefulness – despite the lack of formalities, the mentor and the mentee at the beginning of the program determine the developmental goals that they will work on together to achieve;
3. Involvement – the participants of the program are sincerely interested in achieving the goals;
4. Confidentiality - communication between the mentor and the mentee is based, first of all, on mutual trust, so it is essential that everything that happens during meetings remains only between them and is not transferred to third parties;
5. Investing time – participants devote a sufficient amount of time to the preparation and holding of meetings, as well as to the implementation of mutual agreements;
6. Effectiveness – participation in the program should be beneficial for both mentor and mentee;
7. Openness to learning – the mentor improves their skills while helping the mentee, and the mentee accepts feedback and is open to new experiences;
8. Accessibility – participants are available for communication between meetings;
9. Voluntary – mentor and mentee participate in the program voluntarily and can stop or put on hold their mutual work at any time without any negative consequences for them.

Objectives of the Mentoring Program

1. **Quick inclusion in the workflow**: The objective of the mentoring program is to provide new hires or employees with the guidance and support they need to become productive members of the team quickly. This includes providing them with the necessary training and resources to understand the company's processes and procedures and

2. **Personnel reserve members' leadership potential development**: The mentoring program aims to identify and develop future leaders within the organization. This includes identifying employees with leadership potential and providing them with the training and support they need to develop the skills and knowledge required to take on more senior roles in the company.

3. **Preparation for more complex professional tasks and a higher management level**: The mentoring program is designed to help employees prepare for more complex professional tasks and a higher level of management. This includes providing mentees with the training and guidance to improve their skills and knowledge in project management, problem-solving, and decision-making.

4. **Broadcasting the company's values, strengthening corporate and management culture**: The mentoring program is intended to help employees understand and embrace the company's values and culture. This includes providing mentees

with the opportunity to learn about the company's history, mission, and goals, as well as the values and principles that guide its actions.

5. **Support in career and personal development planning**: The mentoring program aims to provide mentees with support in planning their career and personal development. This includes helping mentees identify their strengths and weaknesses, set goals, and create plans for achieving them.

6. **Developing a holistic understanding of industry, methodologies, and technologies**: The mentoring program is designed to provide mentees with a comprehensive understanding of the industry, methodologies, and technologies used in their field. This includes providing mentees with training and resources to improve their knowledge and skills.

7. **Expanding opportunities for cross-departmental and cross-cultural interaction**: The mentoring program aims to provide mentees with opportunities to interact with employees from other departments and cultures. This includes encouraging mentees to network with other employees and attend cross-functional team meetings and events. This will help mentees to understand the organization as a whole and increase collaboration within the company.

The Corporate Mentor's Toolkit: Transforming Teams and Organizations by Kostiantyn Koptelov

What is the difference between Mentoring and Coaching and Tutoring

What Are the Differences Between Tutoring and Mentoring?

We usually have some confusion between those terms. For example, sometimes people think that tutoring is for ordinary employees, and mentoring is the same, but only for managers.

There is a difference, which is that tutoring is a very direct way to adapt to a new job by learning from a more experienced professional. It's the same person, just more experienced in the same profession. For example, a more experienced sales manager teaches a less experienced sales manager a profession, and a more experienced recruiter trains a less experienced recruiter. This is the most directive type of learning. "You do what I do or what I say."

Tutoring is an excellent way to improve professional skills, especially for young professionals just starting or getting used to a new role in a company. However, tutoring is usually unsuitable for developing mature and experienced employees and managers, as it is the most directive method and leaves no room for another way of doing things. It is not aimed at revealing personal competencies and skills.

There is a distinction to be made between coaching and tutoring.

Coaching is a tool for unlocking the potential of a person. Coaching, as opposed to tutoring, should be as nondirective as possible. A coach may not give instructions, advice, or indications. A coach asks questions without giving advice or sharing their own experience. By asking questions, they can help someone. They help the person find their way to achieve the result while also understanding the obstacles. This can be a very long process. Coach asks questions, and they need much patience. Unlike a tutor, a coach doesn't have to be a professional in the field they are coaching in, and it may even hurt the process if they are. The main thing is good coaching skills, mastery of asking the correct questions at the right time, and patience.

Coaching is an excellent way to help mature specialists and managers grow, especially when we need to find out how practical and resourceful that person is on their own.

Coaching is not suitable for a situation where you need to build up knowledge and competency in a particular area quickly. It is not suitable for immature people because there is nothing for them to lean on. In this case, coaching became psychotherapy, an instrument to deal with a private problem, not a professional one.

So, where does mentoring fit in?

Draw a scale, with tutoring on one side as the most directive instrument and coaching on the other as the most agile and indirective one. You'll see mentoring in the very middle. Of course, you can sometimes act as a tutor when mentoring. Still, you can also use tools for coaching, especially when dealing with internal or intrapersonal barriers.

Roles in the Mentoring Program

Your mentee can be any employee of the organization. If you have any questions about the program, you can talk to Human Resources who will help answer your questions and give you and your mentee the materials you need during the program.

Important: The mentor and mentee do not have to report to the mentee's direct supervisor on how the program is going. Human Resources may get in touch with you to get feedback on the process, solve problems, or get more information to help you communicate better. The content of your meetings with the mentee remains confidential.

Mentor.

1. Participates in the program voluntarily.
2. Chooses a mentee, and determines the number and profile of employees who are ready to develop.
3. Allocates time for regular meetings with the mentee.
4. Advises mentees in difficult professional and managerial situations, including acting for them as a "role model".
5. Analyzes cases from the practice of the mentee.
6. Gives constructive feedback about the personal skills and behavior of the mentee.
7. Inspires to follow the company's values.
8. Forms a broad vision of the industry, methodologies, and technologies.

9. Provides support in career planning and the implementation of an individual development plan.
10. Includes mentees in their network of contacts.

Mentee.

1. Formulates a request for mentoring: goals, topics, and questions to be worked out.
2. Takes responsibility for their development, does not shift it to the mentor or Human Resources.
3. Trusts the mentor's experience and deep understanding of the industry.
4. Actively asks questions and analyzes cases from their practice and the practice of a mentor.
5. Systematically assesses their skills, abilities, and development progress, actively requesting feedback on their development progress from the mentor and other stakeholders.
6. Participates in developmental activities and projects recommended by the mentor to achieve their goal within the program's framework.
7. Shows initiative at the first contact with the mentor when appointing regular meetings within the program's framework.
8. Makes every effort to establish an effective dialogue with the mentor.

Human Resources.

1. Involves mentors in the program.
2. Helps in the formation of a pair of mentor-mentee.
3. Advises mentors and mentees.

4. Monitors the work of pairs mentor-mentee.
5. Provides participants in the program with necessary methodological materials and access to training and events.
6. Monitors satisfaction with the mentoring program.
7. Controls the statistics on mentee progress and the number of mentees on one mentor.

The Corporate Mentor's Toolkit: Transforming Teams and Organizations by Kostiantyn Koptelov

FAQ for mentor

What does a mentor get out of working with a mentee?

1. Transfer of accumulated knowledge, thereby further deepening their understanding.
2. Mutual enrichment of knowledge and skills.
3. Communication with other generations expands the worldview.
4. Development of own leadership potential.
5. Expansion of zones of influence.

What effect does a mentor have?

1. Personal and professional development of the mentee.
2. Career promotion of the mentee.
3. Decisions made by the mentee.

Where can a mentor get helpful information?

1. Books and manuals from HR or the training department.
2. This mentoring book.
3. Consultations with other mentors.
4. Consultation with HR.
5. Company Knowledge Base.
6. Consultations with more experienced colleagues.
7. External training.

Is it possible for a mentor to have their mentor?

Yes, training and self-development in the company are welcome. Moreover, it is much easier for a mentor to do their job when they have a more experienced mentor to consult.

How many mentees can one mentor have?

A mentor can have more than one mentee. However, the mentor's workload and motivation limit the maximum amount. The optimal figure would be 1-3 mentees per mentor.

How does a mentor report on work completed?

A mentor does not have to report to anyone about the progress of the mentoring program. Still, it will be valuable if they sometimes consult with HR or their mentor.

Is it necessary to follow the algorithms and forms in this book?

The forms and algorithms in this book are given as reference material so that the mentor can build on them or use them as a checklist. At the same time, the mentor is free to choose their approaches and tools. We insist that the methods used are moral and fit with the company's corporate culture.

The Corporate Mentor's Toolkit: Transforming Teams and Organizations by Kostiantyn Koptelov

Requests for mentorship and what to do

Requests for mentoring can be completely different.
But we can tell the difference between some of the most common requests for the whole mentoring program or one of the meetings with the mentor.

The following are the most typical requests for mentoring:

Suppose the mentee asks the mentor to talk about their **career development**, such as moving to the next career ladder step. In that case, the mentor may do the following:
   1. Find out from the mentee the desired position or grade.
   2. Help to understand what drives the mentee to make this request (power, recognition, belonging to the team, and the content of the activity).
   3. Figure out what skills and knowledge are needed (the "ideal position profile") for this job.
   4. Compare the actual profile of the mentee (what it is now) and the ideal one. Identify areas for development.
   5. Make a plan to develop specific skills, knowledge, and competencies.
   6. Find opportunities for your mentee that will help them move in the necessary direction: projects, temporary appointments, and so on.
   7. Do a joint analysis of the development results every so often and devise ways to fix things.

If the mentee wants to talk about their **development in general**, the mentor might do one or more of the following:

The Corporate Mentor's Toolkit: Transforming Teams and Organizations by Kostiantyn Koptelov

1. Establish specific developmental goals (What are they? What is the desired development outcome? Timeframe? Resources?).
2. Help in the analysis of the strengths and weaknesses of the mentee and their competencies and skills.
3. Determine how to unite the goals of the organization, the goals of development, and the personal goals of the mentee.
4. Help the mentee develop, keep them motivated, and be there for them when things get hard. Push the mentee out of their comfort zone.
5. Participate in creating a personal development plan (PDP).
6. Keep an eye on how the PDP is being carried out and give your mentee constant, constructive feedback on their development progress and the results they have reached.

One option for the request could be to **talk about new, challenging tasks** that the mentee has been given, especially if they can't handle them.
In this case, the following steps are performed:
1. Understand the complexity of new tasks and in what zone these difficulties are:
    a. in the field of personal qualities;
    b. lack of knowledge and skills;
    c. lack of resources and access;
    d. blocking on some sides.
2. Hold a meeting where you can use the GROW model.
3. Determine what is essential to address these issues:

The Corporate Mentor's Toolkit: Transforming Teams and Organizations by Kostiantyn Koptelov

    a. if there are personal qualities among the problems, then coaching with a professional coach or psychologist is possible,

    b. in case of lack of knowledge, skills - consulting, education, attending training,

    c. In cases of lack of resources, blocking, or access issues, it is possible to use the mentor's contacts to help solve these problems.

4. It can also help to remember and talk about the challenging problems you've solved in the past.

Sometimes, a mentee wants to talk about **issues** when working **with their leader or another coworker**. In this case, you can:

1. Listen to the mentee; be friendly and neutral; do not make your judgment about the colleague. Negative statements about the colleague should not be supported and should be gently suppressed. Instead, ask questions to get the action to move away from the colleague's personality and toward the specific actions and events that make the mentee feel bad.

2. Focus the mentee on their behavior. What precisely in their actions irritates the colleague or causes a misunderstanding?

3. Depending on the specifics, give advice or share your experience with your colleagues at different career stages.

4. Try not to act as a referee or make promises to protect the mentee. Still, you can do this when necessary.

The Corporate Mentor's Toolkit: Transforming Teams and Organizations by Kostiantyn Koptelov

A mentee may come to you to discuss **problems with their subordinates**. The way we can help them is:

1. Determine the essence of the problem:
    a. personality of the mentee;
    b. or "hard subordinate";
    or something else.
2. Use the GROW model.
3. Together, find the causes of the situation and find solutions.
4. Recall and share similar, specific stories from your management experience.

The Corporate Mentor's Toolkit: Transforming Teams and Organizations by Kostiantyn Koptelov

Criteria for the formation of pairs of mentor-mentee

We don't think it's a good idea to pair a subordinate with their immediate boss. This can make the mentoring program less effective and cause a conflict of interest. In addition, not every employee can afford to be completely honest with their supervisor.

The relationship between two people should be beneficial for both parties. For this reason, before selecting a pair, it is essential to interview both parties to find their interests and expected benefits.

To increase the couple's confidence in their ability to be as honest as possible with each other, the mentor and mentee can sign a contract that binds them to a confidential relationship.

Usually, it is better to pair people with similar functional responsibilities and professional experience but, at the same time, different individual qualities. With this option, you can improve people's soft and communication skills, which will add to their professional experience.

It is also a good idea to put together people who have different jobs and experiences but have a lot in common with each other. Such a pairing improves the participants' professional skills and consolidates their strengths.

The ominous options would be a pair of people with similar professional obligations and individual characteristics, or vice versa, with characteristics different from both. In the first case, it will be effortless for them to establish contact and interact, but they will not be able to learn much from each other. In the second case, it will be difficult for them to find common ground.

Key stages of the program

Key stages of the mentoring program:

1. Formation of pairs. The task of the stage is to find the most suitable mentors and mentees.
2. Meet the mentor.
3. Discussion of essential agreements on the format of the interaction of participants for the period of the program.
4. Formulation of main goals for the development of mentee during the program cycle.
5. Completion of the Mentoring Contract (see section "Important forms").
6. Holding regular development meetings. Counseling and analysis of situations that cause difficulties to the mentee.
7. Periodic interim discussion of progress in achieving the goals.
8. The final stage with summing up the results and planning further actions.

The frequency of the interaction

During the program's first meeting, the people involved decide when meetings will be held and how they will be run. The frequency of meetings may vary depending on the current situation. It is important to distribute the interaction throughout the program evenly.

The minimum frequency of meetings is four times a year. The average duration of the meeting is 1–2 hours.

Interaction formats

The following interaction formats are possible:

- In-person live or online meetings,
- Group live or online meetings (one mentor - several mentees),
- Phone or web calls,
- Communication by email,
- Communication in the corporate messenger,
- Joint activities,
- Joint implementation of projects.

Reverse mentoring

In reverse mentoring, a person with less experience, often from a younger generation, helps someone with more experience. This type of mentoring allows for transferring knowledge and skills from a younger, tech-savvy generation to an older, more experienced generation. Reverse mentoring is becoming increasingly popular as companies look for ways to bridge the generational gap and stay current with the latest technologies and trends.

The concept of reverse mentoring originated at General Electric in the late 1990s. The company's CEO, Jack Welch, realized that the company's senior leaders were not as familiar with the latest technologies as the younger employees. To fix this, he set up a program that paired senior leaders with younger employees who were internet, e-commerce, and social media experts. The program was successful, and many other companies have since implemented similar programs.

Reverse mentoring is beneficial for both the mentor and mentee. The mentor, usually younger, gets the chance to share their knowledge and skills with someone with more life experience. They also have the opportunity to develop their leadership and communication skills. The mentee, typically from an older generation, has the opportunity to learn about new technologies and trends and stay current with the industry. They also have the opportunity to develop their own skills and knowledge.

One of the best things about reverse mentoring is the chance to connect people from different generations. In addition, keeping up with the newest innovations and trends is crucial for businesses in today's technological landscape. By setting up a reverse mentoring program, companies can ensure that their senior leaders know about the latest technologies and can make intelligent decisions.

Additionally, reverse mentoring can also create a more inclusive and diverse work environment. It allows individuals from different generations and backgrounds to learn from each other and understand different perspectives.

Implementing a reverse mentoring program can be challenging, and companies must set clear expectations and goals for the program. It's also vital for companies to give the mentor-mentee relationship the resources and tools it needs to work. Online mentoring software can be used to bring mentors and mentees together and give them tools for communication, setting goals, and keeping track of their progress.

In conclusion, reverse mentoring is a powerful organizational and employee development tool. It lets younger people who are good with technology teach older people with more life experience what they know. It also helps bridge the gap between generations and makes the workplace more open and full of different people. Therefore, companies should think about spending money on reverse mentoring programs to keep up with the latest technologies and trends and make sure their senior leaders are well-equipped to make intelligent decisions.

The Corporate Mentor's Toolkit: Transforming Teams and Organizations by Kostiantyn Koptelov

Mentor-mentee interaction

This section will go over various scenarios for mentor-mentee meetings.

Of course, the scenarios that you will find here are given for reference. You have the opportunity to use your own scripts or combine your tools with those that you will learn about in this section. Getting results from a mentoring program is more important than following instructions.

The forms that you will find in this section are not mandatory. Still, they help structure meetings, remember important things, and significantly save time and energy for the mentor and mentee.

Good luck with mastering the scripts.

And, of course, we will be delighted to receive feedback from you on improving our scripts and tools.

The Corporate Mentor's Toolkit: Transforming Teams and Organizations by Kostiantyn Koptelov

The scenario of getting acquainted

The expected duration of the meeting is 1.5–2 hours.

The objectives of the meeting are:

1. Meeting the mentor.
2. Discussion of key agreements on the format of the interaction of participants for the period of the program.
3. Formulation of key goals for the development of mentee during the program cycle.
4. Completion of the developmental contract. See it in the section "Important forms".

Mentor's preparation before the meeting:

We recommend that you familiarize yourself with the information about the mentee that the company's HR will send you in advance. Additionally, you can have a short conversation with the immediate supervisor of the mentee to get feedback about them.

To record plans and arrangements of the program and structure the meeting, you and your mentee can use the "Mentorship Contract," which you can see in the lesson "Important Forms."
Be sure to scan this form.

Since it can be a long time between meetings with the mentee, we suggest you make a separate folder with documents about the mentoring program. This way, when you're getting ready for the next meeting, you can quickly review the most important agreements and conclusions.

Step 1: Acquaintance

1. Briefly tell the mentee about yourself:
    1. The main stages of the career path.
    2. Current work, projects.
    3. Skills and specialization.
2. Ask your mentee to tell you about themself.
    1. How long have they been in the company?
    2. What is their position?
    3. What are the professional plans for the next 3-5 years?
3. Find out their expectations from participating in the program and discuss what kind of help they would like to receive from a mentor and how a mentor can be helpful to them.
4. Share your expectations from participation in the program and the mentee.

Step 2: Discussion of key agreements on the format of interaction

1. Agree with your mentee on the general rules by which you will work throughout the program:
    1. Frequency of meetings.
    2. Duration.
    3. Format.
    4. From whom the initiative to make appointments emanates.

Step 3: Discussion of the Goals of Mentee Development

1. Please discuss with the mentee what goals they would like to achieve during the program. Then, help identify development zones and projects where the mentee could maximize their potential.
2. Discuss what knowledge, skills, abilities, and experience your mentee need to acquire to achieve their goal.
3. Discuss who from their colleagues can help them.
4. Based on your experience, help the mentee identify and prioritize the actions that will give them the desired knowledge, skills, abilities, and experience.

Step 4: End of meeting

1. Ask the mentee to summarize the results of the meeting.
2. Ask them within 1-2 days to send you by email the agreements that you've reached at the meeting if you did not fill out the form directly at the meeting.
3. Set a date for the next appointment.
4. Give homework to the mentee.

Mentor's actions after the meeting

1. Take 5 minutes to record your thoughts.
2. Consult with your HR about possible training and job positions available to your mentee.
3. Browse the training materials available to you and find out which of them might benefit your mentee.
4. If necessary, send the materials.

The Corporate Mentor's Toolkit: Transforming Teams and Organizations by Kostiantyn Koptelov

The scenario of a regular meeting with a mentee

Expected duration of the meeting: 1-2 hours.

Objectives of the meeting

1. Check completed tasks from the last meeting if they were assigned.
2. Working out on current requests of the mentee to the mentor.
3. Discussion of new tasks that the mentee must complete before the next meeting.

Mentor's preparation for the meeting

Take a quick look at and remember the topics you've discussed in previous meetings and what topics you plan to discuss today. To do this, it is convenient to use the form for regular meetings, which you can find in the lesson "Important forms."

Step 1: Beginning

1. Ask the mentee to briefly remind you of what you discussed during the last meeting.
   1. What key topics did we discuss at the last meeting?
   2. What decisions have been taken?

Step 2: Discussion of progress

1. Ask the mentee to remind briefly:

        1. What tasks were set at the last meeting?
        2. What progress has been made on them?
   2. Find out what new things the mentee has learned and what they have realized over the past.
   3. Ask the mentee to talk about progress toward their goal.
   4. Tell them how you assess their success and whether their efforts were sufficient and aimed at achieving the goal.
   5. Discuss possible adjustments in the strategy for achieving the goal of the mentee. New challenges.

Step 3: Choose 1-2 topics to work on during the meeting

   1. Ask the mentee what professional or managerial tasks they are currently facing. Those issues can have no relation with the achievement of their development goal. Instead, find out what causes them the most difficulties in the work.
   2. With the mentee, choose 1-2 main situations you will analyze in detail at today's meeting.

Step 4: Detailed analysis of 1-2 situations that cause difficulties for the mentee

   1. Ask your mentee to describe the situation that causes them difficulties in more detail.
   2. Together, understand the problem in detail:
        1. Identify key barriers,
        2. ineffective mental attitudes,
        3. lack of motivation and its roots,
        4. lack of knowledge, skills,
        5. lack of opportunity to apply knowledge and skills and the reasons for this absence.

3. Recalling your experience and using the mentor's essential skills help the mentee find ways to overcome existing barriers. If the difficulty that has arisen goes beyond your experience and knowledge or capabilities, introduce the mentee to an employee who can help them cope successfully. If the difficulty is associated with the mentee's deeply personal, psychological peculiarities, advise your mentee to find an appropriate specialist, such as a coach, consultant, or psychotherapist. It is advised to involve HR in the search for one.
4. Formulate a specific list of tasks to work out the situation.
5. Ask the mentee how else you can help them. For example, providing support, helping build communication, providing access to information, inviting to training, etc.

Step 5: End of meeting

1. Ask the mentee to summarize the results of the meeting.
2. Offer the mentee homework to develop their skills. See examples of homework for the mentee in section 4 of this book.
3. Thank the mentee for the meeting and set a date for the next one.

Mentor's actions after the meeting

Take 5 minutes to record your thoughts in writing after the meeting. Be sure to note what needs to be discussed next

ns and
Organizations by Kostiantyn Koptelov

time if there are such thoughts. Write down what kind of homework you gave the mentee.

The Corporate Mentor's Toolkit: Transforming Teams and Organizations by Kostiantyn Koptelov

Scenarios of the final meeting to summarize the results of the program

Preparation of the mentor before the meeting

1. Briefly review what you've agreed on at the beginning of the mentoring program
2. Evaluate the results achieved by the mentee during the program. To do this, fill out the "Evaluation of results" form.

Step 1: Greeting

1. Congratulate the mentee on the successful completion of the Mentoring program.
2. Find out their emotions and feelings about participation.

Step 2: Discussion of the Mentoring Program

1. Find out how the mentee evaluates the curriculum and framework of the mentorship program.
2. Get feedback on what can be changed or improved in the program.
3. Make notes for yourself to pass this information on to HR.

Step 3: Discussion of the Results of the Development of the Mentee

1. Discuss how the mentee evaluates the progress on their goal.

2. Show the mentee pre-filled forms with the evaluation of the results.
3. Discuss each other's ratings and comments.
4. Listen to the opinion of the mentee about the results of their development during the mentoring program.
5. Give your assessment of their achievements, and note their significance.
6. Discuss together what lessons should be learned.
7. Discuss the main obstacles your mentee faced and how successfully they have coped with them. Separately, dwell on the goals that have not been achieved during this time. Finally, figure out what resources are missing to perform the planned tasks more efficiently.

Step 4: Discussion of the prospects for the further development of the mentee

1. Ask the mentee exactly how they see their further development.
2. Express your point of view on what, in your opinion, can become a priority for the mentee in the development plan for the next period.
3. Discuss with the mentee if they are interested in further cooperation in the framework of the mentoring program. If necessary, suggest a new mentor for the mentee so that they can develop additional qualities.

Step 5: End of meeting:

1. Sum up the results of joint developmental work during the year.
2. Thank your mentee for working together.

3. Share how you benefited personally from participation in the program.

Mentor's actions after the meeting:

1. Send HR your completed "Evaluation of Results" form.
2. Give HR your and the mentee's thoughts on how the mentoring program is set up and how it could be improved.

Important forms

Forms are essential to a mentoring program because they help the program run smoothly and hold the mentor and mentee accountable for their roles. In this chapter, we will discuss three primary forms: the contract for mentoring, the regular meeting report, and the evaluation of the results of the mentoring program.

Contract for Mentoring

The mentoring contract is a document that defines what both the mentor and the mentee should expect and their responsibilities. This includes the relationship's goals and objectives, the frequency and length of meetings, and any other program expectations or rules. Having a clear and agreed-upon contract makes both parties aware of what is expected of them, and any issues or concerns can be addressed early on.

Regular Meeting Report

Regular meeting reports are used to document the progress of the mentoring relationship. After each meeting, the mentor and the mentee should fill out these reports. They should include a summary of what was discussed, any action items or tasks given, and any feedback or observations. These reports are significant for keeping track of how the mentoring relationship is going and ensuring that both parties work toward the goals and objectives of the contract.

Evaluation of Results

An essential part of any mentoring program is evaluating how well it worked. This evaluation should be done at the end of the mentoring relationship. Both the mentor and the mentee should give their thoughts. The evaluation should look at how well the program worked overall, find places where it could be improved, and make suggestions for future mentoring programs.

In conclusion, the mentoring contract, the report on regular meetings, and the evaluation of results are key forms needed for any mentoring program to work. Organizations can ensure that their mentoring programs help them reach their goals and objectives by setting clear, agreed-upon goals, keeping track of progress, and evaluating the results.

The Corporate Mentor's Toolkit: Transforming Teams and Organizations by Kostiantyn Koptelov

Contract for mentoring

Mentor
Name
Position, department/subdivision
Phone number
Corporate email
Preferred type of communication: | phone | sms | email | messenger |

Mentee
Name
Position, department/subdivision
Phone number
Corporate email
Preferred type of communication: | phone | sms | email | messenger |

Goals for mentoring period

Program Start Date
Expected completion date

Frequency of meetings
Preferred day of the week and time
Format of meetings: | Offline | Telephone | Online |
Format and communication between meetings

Who sends the calendar invitation: | Mentor | Mentee |

The mentee commits to doing homework: | Yes | No |
The mentee is ready to undergo external trainings, attend events: | Yes | No |

How many hours per month the mentee is ready to devote to professional development within the framework of the program

Additional arrangements

The Corporate Mentor's Toolkit: Transforming Teams and Organizations by Kostiantyn Koptelov

Regular mentor-mentee meeting

Date of meeting
Format of meeting

Mentor
Name
Position, department/subdivision
Phone number
Corporate email

Mentee
Name
Position, department/subdivision
Phone number
Corporate email

Goals for the meeting

Tasks from previous meetings | Done?

New tasks to be done before the next meeting

Next meeting date

Summury of the meeting

The Corporate Mentor's Toolkit: Transforming Teams and Organizations by Kostiantyn Koptelov

Evaluation of results of mentorship program

Date of mentoring start
Date mentoring finished

Mentor
Name
Position, department/subdivision
Phone number
Corporate email

Mentee
Name
Position, department/subdivision
Phone number
Corporate email

Number of meetings occurred:

Goals for mentoring program (set at start) — Achieved?

Additional goals set during the program — Achieved?

Mentor's evaluation by Mentee

How do you evaluate Mentee's progress (1 - no progess, 4 - exeptional progress)	1	2	3	4
How effective was Mentee during the meetings? (1 - passive, 4 - proactive)	1	2	3	4
How good Mentee was in making homework? (1 - noting was done, 4 - all tasks were done within the deadlines)	1	2	3	4
Do you see potentian in your Mentee? (1 - not at all, 4 - great potential)	1	2	3	4
Is you mentee ready for new tasks and possible carrer improvement? (1 - not in the nearest year, 4 - fully ready)	1	2	3	4

The Corporate Mentor's Toolkit: Transforming Teams and Organizations by Kostiantyn Koptelov

How much do you get from mentoring for yourself (1 - this was a waste of my time, 4 - mentoring was very usefull for me)	1	2	3	4

What would you like to mention in your Mentee's progress

To what Mentee's features would you like to draw HR's attention in planning his next career steps?

Suggestions on future career for Mentee

Suggestions on next develepmental zones for Mentee

Suggestions on mentorship program improvement

Any additional comments

Examples of homework for mentee's soft skills development

In this section, we'll look at homework options that you can use to develop your mentee's soft skills.
You can do these exercises right in the meeting, discussing the results and the process with the mentee.

You can also suggest that the mentee complete the task after the meeting and send you the result, for example, by email. However, we believe that the best option is a combination in which you once perform an exercise with a mentee in a meeting. And then, give them the task of doing the same exercise with the other case and sending you the result.

The examples you'll see in this section are optional. You can use our exercises. We will also be happy if any improvements to the mentoring program and suggestions for new exercises are passed on to your HR.

Effective communication

Practical communication skills are essential in today's workplace.
Let's see what tasks will help your mentee learn how to communicate correctly and effectively.
Of course, you are not limited to these tasks and exercises and can recommend your own.

Option 1. Let's start the dialogue with the proper preparation

When you start a dialogue, it can be ineffective because you don't have a ready-made plan or a clear strategy. So let's learn how to prepare for an important communication properly.

Stephen Covey, an expert consultant in managing organizations, says that the best way to figure out where you stand is to answer the questions before you talk to someone. You should have a clear vision on such points as:

1. Desired result.
2. Principles and Rules.
3. Resources.
4. Responsibility, control.
5. Consequences.

So, what questions would it be good to prepare answers to before the start of the dialogue?

1. What are my ultimate goals?

2. What are my desired results from the conversation?
3. What rules will I follow when achieving the result?
4. What terms will suit me?
5. What are the limitations when performing this task?
6. What resources do I already have to achieve the desired results?
7. What resources do I need?
8. How will we measure progress and the results achieved?
9. How often will we do this?
10. How will we determine the areas of responsibility?
11. How will we fix the agreements at the end of the conversation?
12. What are the positive consequences if the task is completed?
13. What are the negative consequences if the task is not completed?

Once you have the answers, you're ready. Have a dialogue with your colleagues, considering the preliminary preparation you've done.

Option 2. Reading list

Invite the mentee to read the book and discuss it with you:

1. Barbara Minto, "The Pyramid Principle: Logic in Writing and Thinking"
2. Leil Lowndes, "How to Talk to Anyone"
3. Keith Ferrazzi, "Never Eat Alone"
4. Kerry Patterson, "Crucial Conversations: Tools for Talking When Stakes are High"

When discussing, touch on these things:

The Corporate Mentor's Toolkit: Transforming Teams and Organizations by Kostiantyn Koptelov

1. The main idea of the book.
2. 7-10 Ideas You Remember.
3. 1-2 thoughts on how to put your favorite ideas from the book into practice.

The Corporate Mentor's Toolkit: Transforming Teams and Organizations by Kostiantyn Koptelov

Strategic mindset

Without strategic thinking, it is difficult to imagine a high-ranking leader. But in fact, strategic and system thinking is necessary for employees at all levels: programmers, engineers, architects, and so on.

Now, we'll talk about a few different tasks you can give your mentee to help them learn how to think strategically.

Option 1. Scenario planning

Thinking outside the box is very important because the future is uncertain and can constantly change. Therefore, we recommend that you practice calculating several scenarios for the development of the event.

1. Take some project or goal.
2. Write a project implementation plan.
3. Write down a list of what can go differently.
4. Write several scenarios of how you will achieve results in your project under different conditions. Note that we're not discussing how to mitigate the risks and continue to follow the initial plan. Instead, we're discussing creating several different project scenarios without being tied to the original version.

Option 2. Play games

Master the following strategy boardgames:

- Go
- Chess
- Brass
- Carcassonne
- Catan.

After each game, draw conclusions about what mistakes were made, what strategy you chose, its strengths and weaknesses, and what other strategies you can test in the game.

Option 3. Highlight possible risks

Make lists of possible risks and consequences for each decision within a month or two. Aim to highlight as many factors as possible. Discuss this with the manager and make adjustments. Next, for each possible risk, determine how to minimize its impact on the outcome. Finally, think about a risk mitigation plan.

Option 4. Zoom in

When doing a task, the manager has given you, switch roles often throughout the month. For example, look at this assignment as follows:

1. Artist.
2. Director.
3. Client.
4. User.

The Corporate Mentor's Toolkit: Transforming Teams and Organizations by Kostiantyn Koptelov

Notice what changes for you in viewing the tasks from different angles. What becomes more important and less important during task implementation

Option 5. Reading list

Invite the mentee to read the book and discuss it with you:

- Jamshid Gharajedaghi, "Systems Thinking: Managing Chaos and Complexity: A Platform for Designing Business Architecture"
- Henry Mintzberg, "Strategy Safari: A Guided Tour Through The Wilds of Strategic Management"
- Jim Collins, "Good to Great: Why Some Companies Make the Leap...And Others Don't"
- Nassim Nicholas Taleb, "Antifragile: Things That Gain from Disorder"
- W. Chan Kim, "Blue Ocean Strategy, Expanded Edition: How to Create Uncontested Market Space and Make the Competition Irrelevant"

When discussing, touch on these things:

- The main idea of the book.
- 7-10 Ideas You Remember.
- 1-2 thoughts on how to put your favorite ideas from the book into practice.

Decision making

Let's discuss a few tasks you can give your mentee to develop their decision-making skills.

Option 1. Descartes Square

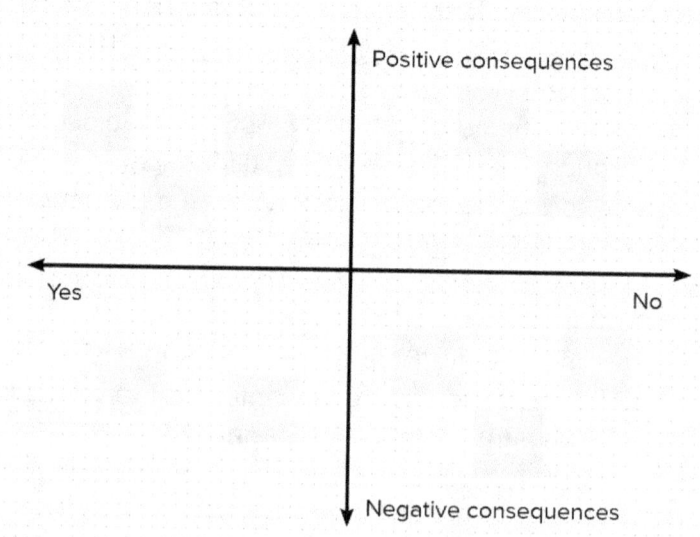

1. Reduce the number of options to one where you can answer "yes" or "no". For example, should an offer of a business trip be accepted?
2. Make a chart with two columns (one for positive decisions (if you'll say "yes") and one for negative one (if you'll say "no") and two rows (one for positive consequences and one for negative). You will have four cells:
    1. positive consequences of a positive decision

2. negative consequences of a positive decision
3. positive consequences of a negative decision
4. negative consequences of a negative decision

3. Discuss what good will happen if you make a positive decision. Fill out respective cell.
4. Determine what good will happen if you dismiss this opportunity. Fill out respective cell.
5. Describe what bad will happen if you agree. Fill out respective cell.
6. Find out what bad will happen if you make a negative decision. Fill out respective cell.
7. Evaluate which solution works best for you.

Option 2. Method of pairwise comparison of solutions

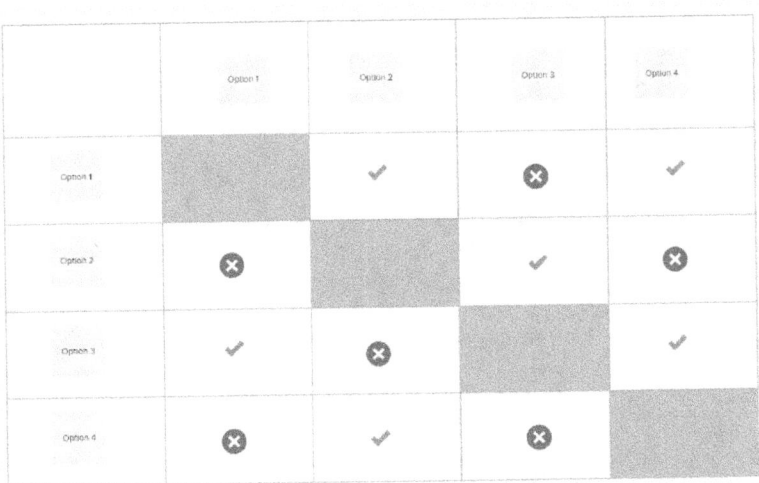

The Corporate Mentor's Toolkit: Transforming Teams and Organizations by Kostiantyn Koptelov

1. List your options.
2. Draw a table in which each row is one solution option.
3. Mirror the options into the column names. As a result, you will get a table with the names of the variants horizontally and vertically the exact names of these variants.
4. Start going through the table from left to right, top to bottom. In each cell compare the options in row and the one in column. Put a checkmark if the option from a row name is better than a one from a column name.
5. Calculate the amount of points for each option.
6. Determine the most priority solution for you.

Option 3. Method of comparing decisions by criteria

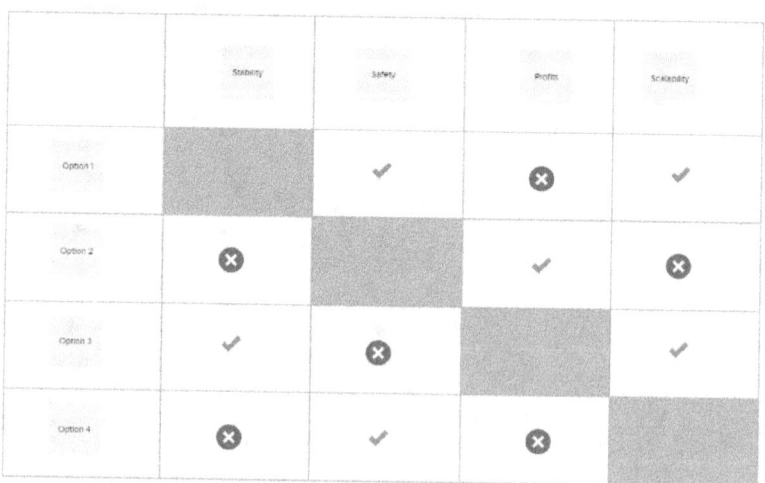

The Corporate Mentor's Toolkit: Transforming Teams and Organizations by Kostiantyn Koptelov

1. List your options.
2. List the criteria that are important when making a decision.
3. Draw a table where the names of the rows are the options for decisions and the names of the columns are the names of the criteria.
4. Start going through the table from left to right, top to bottom and put a checkmark in the cell where the option in row meets the criterion in a column.
5. Identify an option that meets most of the criteria.

Option 4. SWOT Analysis

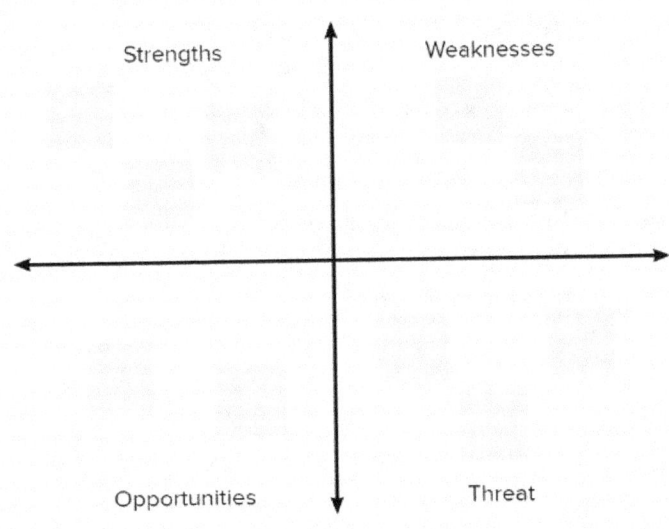

1. Identify the question you want to make a decision about.
2. Define how to:

The Corporate Mentor's Toolkit: Transforming Teams and Organizations by Kostiantyn Koptelov

    1. Make the most of your strengths.
    2. Compensate the weaknesses.
    3. Make the most of your opportunities.
    4. Protect yourself from the possible risks.
3. Assess whether the decision suits you.

Option 5. Reading list

Invite the mentee to read the book and discuss it with you:

- Michael Krogerus, "THE DECISION BOOK"
- Daniel Kahneman, "Thinking, Fast and Slow"
- Chip Heath, "Decisive: How to Make Better Choices in Life and Work"
- David Rock, "Your Brain at Work"

When discussing, touch on these things:

- The main idea of the book.
- 7-10 Ideas You Remember.
- 1-2 thoughts on how to put your favorite ideas from the book into practice.

Public speaking

Let's figure out what tasks can be given to a mentee in order for them to develop their skills of public speaking, presentation, and argumentation.

Option 1. Elevator pitch

Be prepared to present your idea in one minute. If you manage to interest the audience, then it will give you a chance to develop your idea and explain the details.

Step 1. Problem

Formulate briefly (no more than two sentences) what problem you are solving. The problem usually involves the blocking of some process, contradiction, deficit, or loss.

Step 2. Idea

If you had 10-15 seconds for the presentation, in what 1-2 phrases would you describe the essence of your message?

Step 3. Decision

With the help of what solutions, techniques, and tools do you plan to solve the problem, or have you already solved it? Specify one primary solution and no more than two additional ones.

Step 4. Result

Tell us in two sentences what you've done to solve the problem and what you think will happen if we use your solution.

Step 5. Feedback

Get a colleague's opinion about your idea and the presentation. Then, answer the questions, if any.

What is expected from a mentor?

Ask the mentee to present their idea, solution, or project in a minute. Specify the purpose of the speech. Give feedback on how clearly you understood the key message of the speech and whether the goal of the speech was achieved. If you were the decision-maker, how would you react to the speech and why?

Option 2. Learn to answer questions using the principle of "thesis, argument, proof."

Start with an assumption or thesis statement—a short statement on a key topic.
After that, give arguments confirming the truth of the thesis. Then you add the evidence:
- Examples from experience.
- Scientific and statistical data.
- Opinions of reputable experts.
- Links to documents.
- Links to professional literature.

Let's illustrate this task with an example.

Thesis: "It is important for us to implement a task management system in the company."

Argument: "This will allow us to not lose calls and letters from clients, tasks and deadlines from managers, and always keep our finger on the pulse of current projects."

Proof: "Studies have shown that, immediately after the implementation of the task management system, the company's productivity increased by 10%."

Option 3. Analysis of public speaking

Watch five speeches from important speakers in your field and four to five from well-known speakers and public figures in other fields. Pay attention to the factors that make the speaker look convincing:
1. The logic and content of the speech.
2. Body language, facial expressions, and gestures.
3. Interaction with the audience.

Choose one tool from each block. For a month, when speaking in public, focus on one tool, use it, hone it until it becomes a habit for you, and then move on to the next one.

Option 4. Speak

Speak at every opportunity and ask two to three of your colleagues or friends to give you feedback after your public appearances according to the following criteria:

The Corporate Mentor's Toolkit: Transforming Teams and Organizations by Kostiantyn Koptelov

1. How clear is the main idea of the speech, solid arguments, and examples?
2. Whether your gestures, facial expressions, and body language enhance the performance?
3. How confident did you appear?
4. Was your performance convincing?
5. What could have been done better?

Pay attention to repetitive remarks. Determine how you will work on improving your speaking skills.

Option 5. Use Simon Sinek's method

The "golden ring" principle is beneficial when explaining changes in processes, teams, or structures in your company.

1. Explain the purpose and meaning of the change you are proposing. Start with WHY. At the same time, pay attention to talking not about your own meaning, but about the things that are meaningful to the audience.
2. Show a preliminary action plan. It should answer the questions: HOW? WHAT?
3. Involve employees - ask their opinion on what is the best way to act. It should answer the questions: HOW? WHAT?
4. Engage change advocates to take responsibility for specific tasks.
5. Reframe negative comments into a constructive direction. Ask employees, what do they propose to do to avoid the issues if they see any?
6. Answer all questions.
7. Capture all ideas and summarize.

The Corporate Mentor's Toolkit: Transforming Teams and Organizations by Kostiantyn Koptelov

Time management

In this chapter, we'll talk about the options for tasks you can use to improve your mentee's time management skills. Tasks can be performed together with the mentee during the meeting and discussed, or they can be given as homework. In this case, the mentor expects that the mentee will send them the result.

Option 1. Prioritization by importance and urgency

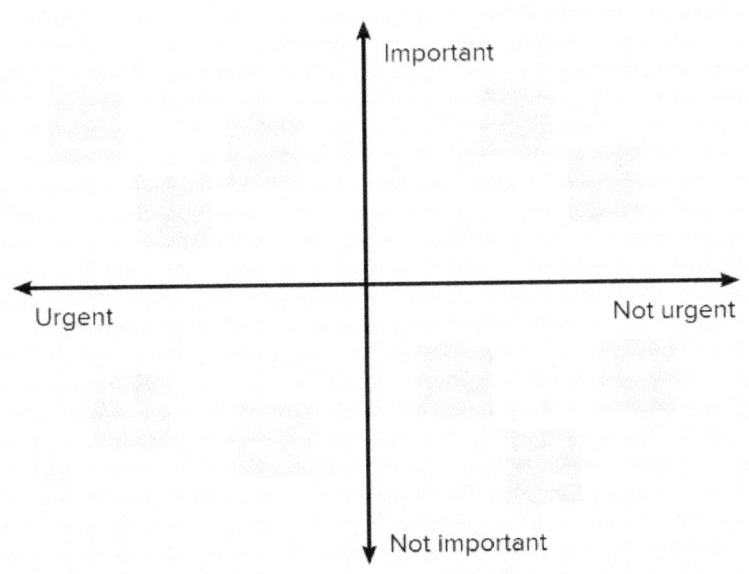

1. Write down all your work tasks.
2. Mark those that:
   a. Important but not urgent.

b. Unimportant and not urgent.
c. Urgent and important.
d. Urgent, but not important.
3. Count the number of tasks in each group.
4. Strive to achieve balance when you have more meaningful and non-urgent tasks in your working plan. These are the strategic tasks that help you make your future better.
5. Use this matrix regularly when planning and deciding what to delegate.

Option 2. Kanban Task Management Board

Wall of Work

Backlog	Doing	Done

The Corporate Mentor's Toolkit: Transforming Teams and Organizations by Kostiantyn Koptelov

1. Think what stages each task goes through. In the simplest variant, they can be "Scheduled - Work in Progress - Done, sent for verification - Completed". A more complicated option: "Planned - Clarify requirements - Design - Develop - Test - Integrate - Ready." Statuses depend on what you do.
2. Create columns with stages. You can use any convenient tool for this (notebook, whiteboard, wall, Trello, Mural and so on). Let's consider for example the most basic option:
    a. Planned - cards with all not started tasks for current projects.
    b. In progress - cards with current tasks on which you are now being working.
    c. Done, sent for review - here are all the tasks that are completed, but require verification by the manager or those who gave you this task.
    d. Completed - fully completed and verified tasks.
3. Take any project and divide it into small tasks. It is convenient when all tasks are approximately equal in execution time.
4. Transfer each task to a card or sticker, depending on which tool you are using. It is convenient when the card has additional information, for example:
    a. Responsible.
    b. Start date
    c. Deadline.
5. Prioritize tasks. The easiest way to do this is to sort them physically, putting the highest priority on the top of the column and the lowest priority on the bottom.
6. Set limits on the number of tasks for individual columns. Setting limits allows you to avoid

overloading resources. For example, the limit for the In Progress column might be three tasks per person or three tasks per column. These restrictions must be negotiated with the team, manager and customer.
7. Make sure that the cards move along the board from left to right as their status changes. The board should be updated regularly on the current status of each task.
8. Measure the average task time. When adding a card to the board, write the start time on it, and when removing it, write the completion time. Use this data to improve the board or your estimations on task completion time when setting goals.
9. Experiment with cards-in-column limits and workflow so that the average task execution time decreases.
10. Conduct retrospective meeting yourself if it is your personal board or with a team. The main task of the retrospective is to analyze the process and results and understand how and what can be improved.

Option 3. Retrospective

Retrospective

What went well	What didn't go well	Actions

1. Write down the tasks in which you made mistakes while planning. The tasks that were:
    a. Not completed on time.
    b. You forgot about the task.
    c. Used more resources than planned.
    d. With a lousy quality result.
    e. Were not performed at all.
2. Analyze what prevented the successful performance. Write down what to
    a. Add to your workflow to make the performance better
    b. Put it away, as it is just wasting your time

c. Or Improve
3. Identify the most recurring causes.
4. Make a plan to fix them. What can be done differently? What resources may you need?

Option 4. Reading list

Invite the mentee to read the book and discuss it with you:

1. David Allen, "Getting Things Done: The Art of Stress-Free Productivity"
2. Stephen R. Covey, "The 7 Habits of Highly Effective People"
3. Jim Benson, "Personal Kanban: Mapping Work | Navigating Life"
4. Brian Tracy, "Time Management"

When discussing, touch on these things:

1. The main idea of the book.
2. 7-10 Ideas You Remember.
3. 1-2 thoughts on how to put your favorite ideas from the book into practice.

Influence

For a manager and someone who is applying for positions at this level, it is very important to be able to exert influence, especially on subordinates. To do this, there are formal tools—for example, the need to obey the one who is higher in the hierarchy—and informal ones, such as charisma.

Let's see what tasks will help your mentee strengthen their skills at influencing others.

Option 1. Analyze the successful experience of your colleagues

1. Choose 3 managers who have authority among employees and management.
2. Ask them to discuss their successful experiences and opinions about what helps them convince people and influence decisions.
3. Write down at least 5 ideas.
4. Study literature and videos about executives you don't know personally.
5. Write down 5 ideas that you think make them influential.
6. Try to implement these 10 ideas into your life.

Option 2. Improve your emotional intelligence

The first step to mastering emotional intelligence and influencing people through it is understanding how they feel. So you need to broaden your view of the range of emotions you can feel.

For 2 months, keep a diary every day in which you answer the following questions:
1. What emotions and feelings did I experience today?
2. What caused them?
3. How did I express them?
4. How did it affect others?
5. How could I express them otherwise?
6. How would this affect others?

Don't be discouraged if, during the first few days of making notes, you see just a few emotions or they are similar from day to day. The main thing is to continue to pay attention to them and write them down in a diary. You yourself will be surprised by the results, especially if you do not take breaks during this exercise.

Option 3. Boost your self-confidence

One of the simplest and, at the same time, most effective ways is the "decide-do" method.

There are many reasons for self-doubt. One of them is that we've got not to follow our decisions, and subconsciously because of this, we cease to trust ourselves.

Try for 30 days as soon as you have made a decision, even the smallest one, and immediately follow it.

Try the described exercise even on small things; for example, I decided to write a letter and immediately sat down to write; when I decided to go to the shower I immediately go.

Option 4. Reading list

Invite the mentee to read the book and discuss it with you:

1. Robert B Cialdini, "Influence: The Psychology of Persuasion"
2. Robin Sharma, "The Leader Who Had No Title: A Modern Fable on Real Success in Business and in Life"
3. Daniel Goleman, "Emotional Intelligence: Why It Can Matter More Than IQ"
4. Robert Greene, "48 Laws of Power"
5. Stephen M .R. Covey, "The SPEED of Trust: The One Thing That Changes Everything"

When discussing, touch on these things:

1. The main idea of the book.
2. 7-10 Ideas You Remember.
3. 1-2 thoughts on how to put your favorite ideas from the book into practice.

Stress management

An essential element of long and productive work are your feelings and comfort. The critical skill here is to learn how to control your stress levels and recover.

If your mentee is a workaholic and you see that they devote too much time to work, what can lead them to burnout? Help them learn how to manage their stress level.

Option 1. Start by planning for rest and recovery

As usual, we fill out our calendar, starting with essential tasks. However, for workaholics, it's best to take the opposite approach.

When planning work time for the next week, tell your mentee to set aside at least 30 minutes each day for rest and leave at least an hour free in case any urgent work arises.

When planning these 30 minutes of rest, determine which rest option they will use (read a favorite book, take a walk around the office, etc.). Then, ask the mentee to determine how this affects their efficiency and productivity. For example, they could compare how many tasks they finish in a week with and without rest plans.

Remember to keep an eye on the mentee because planning a rest does not always equate to actually resting.

Option 2. Analyze stressors and emotional swings

During the week, please give yourself a separate task: observe when you experience the most incredible stress and what caused it during the day. First, mark these events on your calendar. Then, examine your list of what irritates you and what makes you feel better.

For these purposes, it is convenient to use a diary, calendar, or even print out a list of tasks completed during the day and mark those who took energy and gave it.
You can also keep a calendar of emotions.

During the month, describe situations when you could not cope with your own emotions (both negative and positive). Do this as soon as possible after the event to avoid forgetting any details. Then, analyze the situations described and point out the most common things that make you lose your cool. For example, when your decision is criticized, when someone disagrees with you when someone is yelling at you, when you are forced to do something, etc.

For each situation, make a list of alternative actions and how to react in order not to lose your face.

Try out alternative actions in practice.

Tell me about times when you could keep your emotions in check when you usually would have lost your patience and calm. Highlight what helps you deal with emotions.

Option 3. Clarification of meaning

Often, the task causes us stress because we do not like it or do not understand its meaning.

Describe and keep in mind what skills you are developing and what professional development opportunities you receive while solving complex work tasks.

Any task, even the most boring one, can be turned into a way to become better.

For example, when I had to write boring work reports, I focused on how to get my ideas across in as few words as possible without sacrificing quality. I kept statistics on this, which strengthened my writing communication skills while doing a task that was routine and not initially intended for self-development.

Option 4. Prepare for stress

Our work is non-linear. There are periods of high load and periods of calm.

Analyze, together with the mentee, the schedule of their tasks for the month ahead and highlight the most stressful periods (completion of milestones, overlapping several tasks, etc.). Plan more "free time" these days and try to redistribute fewer and fewer critical tasks to other periods. At the end of the period, think about how well you dealt with the situation.

The Corporate Mentor's Toolkit: Transforming Teams and Organizations by Kostiantyn Koptelov

Ask the mentee what helped them cope with stress during peak periods, how they redistributed tasks, and whether the mentee will apply the approach in the future.

Option 5. Finding your way to work with stress

Study the literature, watch videos, chat with colleagues and acquaintances, and write down at least 10 ways people cope with stress. For example, go to the gym, meditate, draw something on paper, switch attention to the positive, etc. Then, devote one day to trying out one of the prescribed options. Examine the results in your mood. Repeat until you've identified the top 2-3 stress-relieving techniques.

Key mentoring skills

The role of a mentor requires specific skills.

In this section, we will figure out what skills a mentor should have and how to develop them.

You will get a set of algorithms for acting in a particular situation to help your mentee grow effectively.

We recommend that you improve all your skills, even the ones you are good at, by focusing on one per month. And, of course, you can use the lessons ad hoc, just when you need to use this or that tool in a meeting with a mentee.

Good luck with mastering the skills of a top-level mentor!

The Corporate Mentor's Toolkit: Transforming Teams and Organizations by Kostiantyn Koptelov

Making contact

Building trust with your mentee before you can have productive conversations with them would be best.

People sometimes say that making contact is like the first serve in a game, which sets the tone for the rest of the game. The main goal of making contact is to set up a good, friendly environment for future interactions.

What is crucial to establishing contact?
1. Readiness for a contact.
2. Interest in a partner.
3. Openness.
4. Equality of positions in the conversation, lack of pressure "from above".

To establish contact, it is necessary to demonstrate respect, a positive attitude, and a sincere interest in your mentee in all possible ways:
1. In words.
2. In gestures.
3. In actions.

The first impression is formed in the first 20–40 seconds of conversation. After that, we evaluate each other's appearance, friendliness, speaking ability, first words, and actions. In the first minute, a person cannot determine how competent a colleague is. But it is easy to pay attention to non-verbal symbols: gestures, facial expressions, and eye contact. Use them to show unobtrusiveness, a desire to be helpful, and strengthen everything you say.

What to do:
1. Make eye contact.
2. Greet mentee by name.
3. Introduce yourself.
4. Smile sincerely and warmly.

Find out how to call your mentee

"Good afternoon, Michael; tell me whether you prefer to be addressed by your full name or your shorter one."

Compliment

For example: "Beautiful shirt, it suits you."

Suggest an alternative

For example, "Will it be more convenient for you to communicate in the meeting room or on the street in an informal setting?"

Immediately identify the benefit

For example, "I have good experience in architecture, so you have a good chance to improve your skills and knowledge in it."

Active listening

"Active listening" is a behavior that allows you to understand the interlocutor adequately and, at the same time, show them your attention and goodwill. Active listening increases communication effectiveness and avoids misunderstandings, conflicts, and mistakes.

It is important not only to hear and understand the interlocutor but also to show them sincere interest. Therefore, getting all the critical information from the conversation is essential without changing it.

The technique is based on the other person's active participation in the conversation, where the focus is on the meaning of words, intonation, mood, facial expression, and gestures simultaneously. Our task is to scan the mentee, read their mood, and then use the proper techniques.

Active Listening Techniques

Ask clarifying questions. This will help you better understand the mentee if they forget to tell you something. As a result, you will avoid blunders and misunderstandings.

For example: "Michael, you said the report would be ready on the 19th of August. So let's clarify: in the morning or the evening? And by what time should I wait for it to make room to work with it on my calendar?"

Sincerely worry about the mentee's problems, involve them in the conversation, listen carefully, and empathize with the interlocutor. Show that you want to help the mentee. Use these techniques and manage the conversation on behalf of the listener.

For example: "Mike, I'm perturbed about your project. I follow the progress of the implementation. It hurts me to hear that deadlines are missing".

Develop your thoughts. If there is a slight innuendo, follow the logic of the mentee and arrange the thought for them. You will be able to get the conversation back on track and encourage the mentee to talk more about the subject.

For example: "John, we discussed that you would like to develop certain soft skills. To accomplish this, you will send me a list of training you wish to attend so I can help approve them. Should I expect a list from you via mail or the corporate messenger?"

Make pauses in the conversation; they help the interlocutor to gather their thoughts and not forget important details.

For example: "Ron, here's the presentation; take a minute. And I'm off to our kitchen for some coffee. How much sugar do you want?"

Use attentive silence—the ability to listen carefully, showing interest, and not interrupting.

Use the echo response. This is a technique for authentically repeating accented words, often with surprise. The mentee sees: that the conversation is interesting to you, so they become more open and ready to develop the topic.

For example:
Mentee says: "Imagine they said we don't use tabs; just a double space at the beginning of the line while programming. Like, there's no such thing in manuals!"
You say: "There's no such thing in manuals? Well, come on, the coding standard says you should do that!"

Paraphrase. Repeat their thoughts in your own words. They will understand that you understood them correctly and will feel the trust.
For example: "In other words, you believe that..."

Make abstract. Draw a line under the conversation. If there are disagreements, make comments on this.
For example: "Harry, I think we understood each other. I'll call you back when there are relocation vacancies to other offices."

Developmental feedback

Feedback is when you tell someone about their past actions in the present, hoping it will change how they act. Giving feedback allows the person to see themselves from the outside in a particular situation. You allow them to understand and feel their actions' effects, reactions, and results.

Principles of developmental feedback:

1. **Timely**: Refers to a recent situation that is still fresh in the memory of you and your mentee.
2. **Specific**: Refers to specific events, situations, and behaviors.
3. **Focused**: Limited in the number of topics, centered around one or two key areas, not trying to cover too many questions at once.
4. **Based on facts**: Avoids generalizations. Leaves no room for ambiguity.
5. **Descriptive**: Describes behavior, does not label the person.
6. **Balanced**: If there are both examples of successful patterns and reasons for improving a person's behavior. Talk about both without focusing only on examples of ineffective behavior.
7. **Constructive**: Leads to a discussion of future actions and possible behaviors. A good outcome of feedback is your mentee's declaration of future actions, a to-do list, or a request for assistance.

8. **One-on-one**: This does not imply the presence of third parties, especially in the case of negative feedback.
9. **Personal**: Emphasize that you are expressing your personal opinion.
10. **Dialogue**: The mentor necessarily asks questions to reveal the mentee's perception of the situation and clarify their motives and reasons.

Feedback schemes

Feedback is given in two cases: when a person did everything right, and it is necessary to consolidate such behavior and inspire further productive work, and when something was done incorrectly and required correction. We use different algorithms for these options. I want to stress the importance of giving positive feedback often and avoiding making mistakes when the mentor only gives corrective feedback.

To consolidate a favorable situation:

Step 1: Describe the situation you would like to discuss.

Step 2: Emphasize what was done well by the mentee, observing feedback principles.

Step 3: Clarify any questions the mentee may have.

Example: "Hey, John, I've received your report. I noted that you sent it on time, and I appreciate how many details were given in the third clause. It seems you worked very hard on this report. Do you have any questions for me in the meantime"

To correct a negative situation:

Step 1: Describe the situation you would like to discuss.

Step 2: Ask your mentee to evaluate their actions.

Step 3. Give your opinion of the mentee's actions, observing feedback principles.

Step 4. Together with your mentee, work on the CAPA plan. This is a Corrective and Preventive Actions plan to correct the situation and prevent any possible recurrence.

Example dialogue:

- Hey, John, I've received your report. Unfortunately, it was beyond the schedule and, in my opinion, was too general. What do you think about this situation?
- I started working on the report too late, so I did it at night. So possibly it is not the best report I could write.
- Okay, let's think about the CAPA plan
- Okay, to correct this situation, I would work hard on this report to make it better and more detailed, and to prevent this in the future, I am going to put a deadline for such reports in my calendar a day before the actual one, to have enough time for a revision.
- Sounds good. I'm waiting for your revised report today.

Reframing

Reframing is a positive reformulation.

"Reframing" means "changing the framework," presenting the situation in a different, more advantageous light. You can always find a way to make even the worst things that happen to you seem okay and essential for your development and growth.

Let's say a person has failed on an important business project. What's good about that? In any case, now they have experience and knowledge of how not to act. This increases the likelihood of success for future projects.

Mentors use this technique very often for a variety of tasks, including:

1. To motivate a person to develop.
2. To change their attitude, attitude to skills, and actions.
3. To draw valuable conclusions from failures, etc.
4. As an effective response to doubts and objections.
5. To help a person find positive content in their past negative experiences and new opportunities for further development and achievement of results in the future.

There are several ways to use reframing:

1. Context reframing.
2. Showing the other side.
3. Reframing with "But".

4. Reframing with connotations.
5. Use of an alternative question.

Context reframing

If you change the context of the message, the approach to the content also changes. The same behavior can be beneficial in one situation and harmful in another. When reframing a context, we look for a situation where this behavior will have a different meaning.

Example:
- "A Person Who Reports Misconduct of Others Is Not Worthy of Respect".
- "Wait, if they reported a violation of safety rules, they did save someone from a possible injury".

Showing the other side

Most of us think of stereotypes. In business, there are also many common stereotypes. It is essential to be able to destroy them with the help of reframing.

Example:
High Price - Quality Stuff Can't Be Cheap
It's a long time to deal with - You become a valuable employee because you know that others don't
Too short a time to complete the project - A way to learn how to make a minimum viable product in practice.

Reframing with "But"

From a technical standpoint, the simplest reframing option is to use the word "but" to compensate for the weak.

Example:
My monitor is too small, but it saves space on my work table and provides sharper image resolution.
The methodology is too complex but possesses many possibilities.

Reframing with connotations

Connotation is the evaluative component of a word.
Synonyms can have different emotional colors. For instance, "our agent" is seen as a good thing, while "their spy" is seen as a bad thing, even though both words mean the same thing. We need to choose formulations that will give the partner more benefits.

Example:
Stingy - Lean
Fickle - Creative.

Use of an alternative question

We ask alternative questions using the contrast effect. This technique allows you to emphasize what the partner should pay attention to in the first place.

Example:
Would you like to learn a new skill or just be able to pretend you have one?

The Corporate Mentor's Toolkit: Transforming Teams and Organizations by Kostiantyn Koptelov

Asking developmental questions

People learn better when they find answers to their questions and do not receive ready-made solutions. Therefore, a mentor's most important skill is asking questions that allow a person to come to a solution independently. For example, you can use the GROW coaching model, built on questions. For more information about this model, see the lesson "Assistance in Development Planning."

The question invites the mentee to search in a particular direction, for example, by looking within themselves or into the future. Effective questions catch you off guard because they are unexpected or even incredible. Sometimes the most compelling questions are the ones that sound the stupidest. Sometimes it can even be, "I don't know what next question to ask you now; what about you?"

The mentor needs to observe which issues fall into emotionally significant areas for the mentee. The ability to pick the best question is a skill, and it is trained over time!

An excellent developmental question is:

1. simple,
2. medium size,
3. one idea at a time,
4. impartial,
5. without tricks and provocations,
6. makes you think, opening an internal dialogue,
7. helps to build a personal strategy for success.

It is worth refraining from
1. questions containing an answer and leading
2. meaningless questions where the context is omitted
3. emotional or judgmental, such as "do I need to explain this obvious thing?"

Examples of questions

Reveal the thinking of the mentee. Determine what they like best and are successful in.
1. What type of tasks brings you the most pleasure?
2. Tell us why do you think this is an ideal professional result?

Set Direction.
1. What will be the most significant result of our meeting?

Clarify values.
1. Why is it essential for you to achieve your goal?
2. How will this goal achievement help others?

Enable motivation.
1. What do you think motivates you best?
2. What is the best way for you to support yourself at this stage?
3. Some things need to be done; otherwise the situation will change for the worse. How should you take care of them?

Define success criteria.
1. How will you know you've achieved what you want?

Enable creativity.
1. Imagine that there is a person who managed to cope with a similar situation, what would they do differently?

Make and prioritize a plan.
1. What will be the first step, where should you start?
2. If you had all the resources you needed now, what would you do first?

Work out obstacles along the way.
1. What can stop you?
2. What kind of help is needed?
3. What obstacles can be encountered on the way?
4. How do you stay motivated for the rest of the trip?

Develop mindfulness.
1. How do you feel yourself now?
2. What are you doing now?
3. How does this move you towards your goal?
4. Is that the right thing that needs to be done?

Gain experience and work on bugs.
1. What could have been done differently?
2. What have you learned?

Learn more than you planned.
1. I don't know what next question to ask you now, what about you?

Seeing what the mentee hides from themselves.
1. What solution are you trying to avoid?
2. What are you missing out on here?

Ability to explain and instruct clearly

As a mentor, you will have to explain and instruct a lot. It is essential to learn how to do this as clearly as possible. This will allow you to save time and nerves. Of course, this skill develops with practice.

The basic principles are simple:

1. Structure the information
2. Get regular feedback from the mentee. Ideally, after each logical block, it is essential to pause and clarify what questions your mentee has.
3. If possible, visualize, illustrate, give examples.
4. At the end, sum up, repeat the main points or ask the mentee to do it.

Let's find out how to structure information.

The principle of hierarchy (the pyramid)

Do not give the interlocutor information on the principle of "all at once." To be adequately understood, adhere to the hierarchy in the presentation of information. First, describe the essence of the question. Then, highlight the main details. And only then should you draw each detail separately.

The critical mistake here is to immediately start explaining the details and delving into them without going through the highest level. As a result, structured information is perceived more easily. And this structure can be imagined in the form of a pyramid.

For example, to describe a software product, we start with an enumeration with a short explanation of which modules are included in it and what connections there are between them, and only after the upper level has been explained, we descend to the details of the implementation of each module.

The principle of "starting from the needs of the mentee"

Start the story with what your listener is interested in—their questions, opportunities, or challenges.

For example:
"In order to get a raise, it is important to show good results at the end of the year. To do this, let's go through your goals and figure out which way to achieve them will be optimal."

The principle of "from bump to bump"

If we need to discuss something unfamiliar, complex, or containing scientific terminology, we do not jump right into details and terminology. Instead, we start it with something close and understandable for the mentee. You can think of this as if we were moving to the other side of the swamp. We'd jump over to the nearest bump, secure ourselves, and then jump on.

The Corporate Mentor's Toolkit: Transforming Teams and Organizations by Kostiantyn Koptelov

The principle of "thesis - argument - proof"

First, you put forward an assumption or a thesis. Then you expand it, and only then do you add evidence.

For example:
Thesis: "Developing soft skills is important".
Argument: "The ability to present, speak, structure information, manage time makes an employee much more effective and develops emotional intelligence".
Proof: "Scientists have found that managers who regularly engage in self-development are 45% more likely to receive a promotion".

Let's sum up.

1. The main thing is practice. The more and more often you explain, the easier it is for you to do so.
2. Before you start telling, structure the information to make it more straightforward.
3. Remember that there is always a chance to be misunderstood, so constantly clarify what and how the mentee understood. Then, ask in your own words to retell.
4. Use as many examples and illustrations as possible.
5. Summarize.

Setting developmental goals

This skill consists of several particular skills.

1. The ability to correctly formulate any goals, for example, using SMART or OKR approach.
2. Ability to find those development goals that precisely:
   1. Will propel a person to achieving their life goals (both professional and personal).
   2. Will be of interest to them.
   3. Will be in «zone of nearest development» (i.e. will be difficult, but feasible).

The mentor helps to formulate developmental goals during almost every session. These can be both long-term development goals (for several years, for a year), and short-term (a goal for a specific session, until the next session, for a month).

SMART model

SMART is a well-established tool that you can use to plan and achieve goals. Although, there are different options for deciphering the abbreviation, we will talk about the one in which the goal should be: Specific, Measurable, Achievable, Relevant and Time-bound.

Specific
The goal should tell you what to do and how to do it. It should be clear and specific so you can focus on getting it done instead of trying to figure out what it means.

For example, make a presentation about the month's work in the department.

Measurable
Goals should be measurable to track progress towards them.
For example, prepare a presentation on 15 slides about the results of the department's work for the month.

Achievable
The goal must be achievable. Whether or not you can reach a goal depends on your experience, resources, and limitations.
For example, make a 15-slide presentation about the results of the department's work for the month based on the reports of employees and materials already made by the statistics department.

Relevant
The reason for the goal should be apparent to the one who achieves it. But unfortunately, people sabotage meaningless goals and tick off those that are not significant.
For example, to increase the budget for the next month, make a 15-slide presentation about the results of the department's work for the month.

Time-bound
If the goal does not have a clearly defined completion date, then it will be done forever; there will always be something of higher priority.
For example, prepare a 15-slide presentation on the results of the department's work for the month for the general meeting on Thursday at 4 p.m.

OKR Model

OKR makes it very convenient to track progress towards a goal by splitting it into two blocks: the goal itself and the progress meters towards it.

In this technique, the goal consists of two blocks.

Objective: It should inspire, be meaningful and understandable, and be close to the employee.
For example, speak at an international conference on behalf of a company.

And three to five **key results** to track progress toward the goal.
The mistake will be to confuse the key results and stages of the project. This is because the stages of the project are executed sequentially, one after another, and the key results in OKR can change in parallel.
All key results should be measurable, and the mentee should be able to track them on a weekly basis. Please try to avoid binary key results, as they make no sense.

For example:
Objective: Speak at an international conference on behalf of the company.
- Key Result 1: Take 10 lessons from the Public Speaking book.
- Key Result 2: Prepare a presentation on 15 slides.
- Key Result 3: Arrange participation and transfer.
- Key Result 4: Conduct 10 rehearsals of the performance.

Assistance in development planning

To help a person make a high-quality development plan, it is necessary to know what developmental actions can be, how to choose the type of developmental activities, and how to combine them correctly.

When assisting in drawing up a plan, it is vital not to make a plan for your mentee but to help them do it independently.

It is possible and necessary to suggest ways to develop, ways to look for ways to develop, and ways to get people to think creatively. However, it makes sense to share your opinion only when your mentee has fully used all their ideas.

The GROW model can be helpful.

"G" stands for Goal. Setting goals and aligning expectations.
"R" stands for Reality. Investigation of the current situation and problems.
"O" stands for Options. Finding the barriers; development and analysis of possible actions to overcome obstacles.
"W" stands for Way forward. Drawing up an action plan.

Stage GOAL

Setting goals and aligning expectations.

The mentor helps the partner make a plan for how the project will turn out, considering the partner's external reality and expectations. The most important thing here is to determine the condition for fulfilling the goal and the checklist by which we will understand when the goal will be achieved.

Use the lesson "Setting developmental goals."

The Corporate Mentor's Toolkit: Transforming Teams and Organizations by Kostiantyn Koptelov

Stage REALITY

Investigation of the current situation and problems.
Mentors ask questions and actively listen, trying to understand:
1. Facts about the current situation or problem.
2. Partner's attitude to the situation or problem.
3. Partner's intentions.

Use the lesson materials on "Asking developmental questions."

The mentor tries to show as accurately and in as much detail as possible what the partner did and how they thought about what they did. In addition, the mentor attempts to understand what is preventing the partner from achieving the goal and assists them in realizing the situation and their internal and external obstacles.

Examples of questions:
1. What do you want to discuss?
2. What result do you want to achieve?
3. What do you expect from our meeting?
4. What do you expect from me?
5. How much time do we have?

We move on as soon as the partner has figured out what they want to get out of the meeting and what they expect.

1. Describe the situation.
2. What happened?
3. What steps or actions have you taken or planned to take?
4. What are the results?
5. What stopped you from doing more?

6. Is there anything else that can be done?
7. What result did you want to achieve?
8. What are the obstacles in the way forward?
9. What hindered or may hinder you?
10. What are you particularly concerned about?
11. What can you influence in this situation, what can't?
12. Who else controls or influences the situation?
13. What resources do you have (experience, time, support, people, etc.)?
14. What resources are you missing? What can be their sources?

Let's move on once the partner and mentor have explored the situation together and identified the external and internal obstacles to the goal and their respective responsibilities and contributions to the situation.

Stage OPTIONS/OBSTACLES

Development and analysis of possible actions to overcome obstacles.

The mentor asks questions and uses other methods to get the partner to think about what they could do to solve the problem and how they could do it.

Examples of questions:
- How do you see your actions to solve this problem? What are the possibilities?
- What have you/others done in similar situations before (if there are precedents for successful resolution of such problems)?
- If you could improve or change the situation, how would you do it?

- Remember a person from the circle of your acquaintances, successful in solving such problems. If they were you, what would they most likely do?
- If you were an outside observer, what would you recommend doing?
- Let's list alternative actions, as well as their pros and cons.
- If you had all the resources you needed, what would you do?
- Let's work together on possible solutions.

The stage is over when the partner has come up with and analyzed a list of possible actions for getting around problems and reaching the goal, as well as chosen the direction of future actions.

Stage WAY FORWARD

Drawing up an action plan.
The mentor helps the partner plan specific actions and checks the plan to make sure it works "in real life."

Examples of questions:
1. Let's draw up a plan of action.
2. What exactly will you do?
3. When?
4. What could stop you?
5. How do you overcome that?
6. What resources are needed?
7. Whose approval/help do you need?
8. Who, what, and when exactly will do it?
9. Will the plan be feasible? First, assess your readiness to act in the chosen direction on a 10-point

scale (if the readiness is less than 7, the commitment to the adopted plan is low).
10. Rate your confidence in success on a 10-point scale. What can you do to increase your confidence?
11. On the basis of what intermediate results will you judge the success of your actions?
12. How are you going to track the implementation of the plan?

The stage is over when the partner has made a plan with clear deadlines, steps, resources, and an end result that can be measured. In addition, the partner demonstrated confidence in and commitment to the developed plan.

Mentor and mentee agree on what specific tasks from the plan should be completed by the next meeting, as well as on deadlines.

The next meeting with the mentor always begins with an overview of what has been done, what could have been done better, and, if something has not been done, what the reasons are and what to do to ensure that everything is done by the next meeting.

Ability to inspire and challenge

It is essential for a mentor not only to transfer knowledge but also to inspire the mentee for personal and professional growth, as well as to challenge them so that they can achieve much more than they are used to. Let's discuss a few tactics on how to achieve this.

Tactic 1: Help the mentee feel the meaning of the work

People work better if they do it meaningfully. You can also use meaning to inspire people and make them supporters of your projects and goals.

Adam Grant, a professor at the Wharton School of Business, and his colleagues did an experiment with students who get donations from graduates. Students called people for hours and listened to refusals again and again, which greatly demotivated them. Something had to change. The head held a meeting and showed the letters of students who received scholarships with the help of donations. They then invited a fellow who shared how the opportunity to go to university changed their life. "When you talk to someone on the phone, every time you remember that there is someone in this world who relies on you," was the main thought. A month later, the medium amount of contributions for the week increased from 185.94 dollars to 503.22 dollars. By giving people a sense of the meaning of their work, you get significantly more engagement and efficiency.

Tactic 2. Communicate

The easiest and most obvious way to motivate a person is to communicate personally, encourage, inspire, and listen. Employees usually like it when top managers pay attention to their ideas, support them, and can quickly start a conversation. Everything you say and does motivate or demotivates your colleagues in some way. Attention, respect, gratitude, and care for them are necessary qualities.

Tactic 3. Maintain corporate culture and traditions

Corporate culture is created in good times to help survive in bad times and in better times to grow and scale faster. First, take the time to tell your mentee how things work in the company. What are the rules, why are they precisely the way they are, what is behind our corporate values, and what culture do we have? Then, involve them in informal company events.

A sense of unity and cohesion not only increases productivity but also serves as an excellent preventive measure against stress and burnout.

Tactic 4. Explain and, at the same time, give emotions

Not all emotions work the same way. To inspire people and enlist their support, we can use opposite emotions.

For example, the manager was tasked with reducing their department's budgets. As a result, they stopped giving out free coffee and cookies at work, which was criticized in the smoking room. They would have gained understanding if they had used our tactics and first talked to employees, making them feel sad about the size of the bonuses now and then giving them a sense of hope about what bonuses might become if they cut costs.

This is a very effective strategy, but you need to be careful with it and use it in an honest way if you want to inspire people instead of trick them. We strictly don't use the principle of "doing bad things to get everyone upset and then canceling them to make them happy."

Tactic 5. Use the SCARF pyramid

Many have heard of Maslow's pyramid of needs." And there are a lot of questions about it because people actually often sacrifice the values at the base of the pyramid (like security) for higher values. This is confirmed by firefighters, rescuers, military personnel, and volunteers.

SCARF is a much more effective needs assessment model. SCARF stands for Fairness, Relatedness, Autonomy, Certainty, Status.

It is based on **Fairness**. For the sake of a sense of fairness, people are willing to sacrifice a lot. And it's important for the mentor and manager to check on the mentee often to see if the principle of fairness is being broken.

Further, it is vital for the employee to have a sense of **Relatedness** and belonging to any social group. By involving the mentee in work and informal groups and activities, we increase their sense of calm and pleasure from working with us.

The next level is **Autonomy**. Of course, people appreciate being given some level of autonomy. But at the same time, they need support and to not be thrown one-on-one with problems.

Then there is a sense of **Certainty**. Confidence in yourself as a professional, in a department, in a manager, in a company, in a niche.

And at the very top is **status**, its attributes, and the opportunities that it provides.

Final words

Congratulations!

You finished the book, and now you have all the qualities and skills you need to be a top-level mentor in your company!

Of course, you'll need some time to make them better and develop the skills into habits, but you've already put in a really big effort going through this book.

I hope that you will enjoy helping people reach their developmental goals.

And remember to ask questions, add comments, and leave feedback on this book.

You can find me at www.koptelov.org or send me an email at mail@koptelov.org.

Have good luck being a mentor!

www.ingramcontent.com/pod-product-compliance
Lightning Source LLC
Chambersburg PA
CBHW070244220526
45465CB00004B/1517